My Journey with JAMES

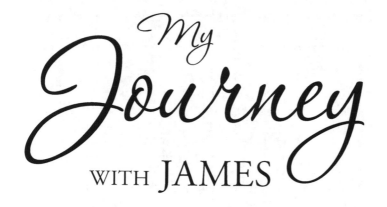

Verse-By-Verse Discoveries

ABIGAIL J. ENWHITE

WestBow Press
A Division of Thomas Nelson

WestBow Press books may be ordered through booksellers or by contacting:

WestBow Press
A Division of Thomas Nelson
1663 Liberty Drive
Bloomington, IN 47403
www.westbowpress.com
1-(866) 928-1240

ISBN: 978-1-4497-8630-4 (sc)
ISBN: 978-1-4497-8631-1 (e)

Library of Congress Control Number: 2013903281

Printed in the United States of America

WestBow Press rev. date: 03/26/2013

Credits and Thanks to:

* **Spirit Filled Life Bible**
1991 Thomas Nelson, Inc.

** **David and Brenda Strait**
Bible ministry Molalla Foursquare Church 2009

*** **Paraphrased Living Bible cross-references** and helps 1971 by Tyndale House Publisher, Wheaton, Illinois 6018 All used by permission.

+ And number by a word means **definition**
from computer thesauruses
Or **answers** to the blank on page 58

Dedicated to:

All my grandchildren
as well as all
those wishing to learn
what it means to
be a Bondservant of
Jesus Christ!

My consecration prayer for this trip/journey
Heavenly Father,

You have said if anyone lacks wisdom to ask of you and it will be given to whomsoever asks. Well, Lord, I am asking for that wisdom as you guide me into writing this work manual of James. May it help New Babes in Christ, Teenager or anybody wishing to know what a true Christian, or bondservant is. Guide them in finding their answers while taking this journey through the book of James. Give them boldness to walk out the good news of Your Word, helping fellow travelers to be challenged also. Father , make it an enjoyable journey as well as bring encouragement to each traveler. Finding fresh nuggets of treasures for the rest of their live.

Thank you Father for your wisdom freely
given to this writing and study.

Amen!

Enjoy your journey with
James

My name is ______________________________

I started this study with ______________________________(group)

On this date: ______________________________

[This part of page to be filled out by instructor/teacher, or parent.
Only if it is a self-done study will you complete this area

Congratulations are in order:

You have persevered on this journey and finished this course
On ______ day of in the year ______ of your Lord ______

Table of Contents

Introduction to our journey

WELCOME TO A JOURNEY with James and growth in your practical walk with Jesus! You want to know who you are in Christ? What is a real Christian, or what is a true Religion? James is a good place to get those questions answered, so lets get our journey and new discoveries underway.

You may be asking, why James? Who else would know the walk/ journey better than James, after all he grew up with Jesus! Yes, this is James the brother of Jesus. In the New Testament there are three different men with the name James. They are James the son of Zebedee, James, the son of Alphaeus, and this one, known as James the Great, the brother of Jesus. James makes the words *faith, riches, handling the tongue, pride, and prayer* very clear. James was not a theologian, but a practical man, teaching reality in walking the Christ like walk. James was a man that began his walk in Acts 1:13.

Don't look for doctrine in this book of James, it is completely and primarily a practical man infused by the Holy Spirit to write a letter to the Jews that had scattered over the different areas, as well as Christians today. I love James, because he is a practical writer, who instills Godly living rather than religious theories.

Now that we have established who James is and what his purpose was for writing let's **get digging for nuggets.** Put on your eyes of **reality, practicality, and simplicity.**

Chapter One

Let's get digging!

*Verse one: *"James, a bondservant of God and of the Lord Jesus Christ. To the twelve tribes which are scattered abroad. Greetings".* James calls himself a bondservant of God to the Lord Jesus Christ. What is a bondservant to you? Lets break it down since this is a compound word. Bond, the dictionary says it's a tie, linked, connected, a union, attachment, relationship and friendship. – That is simple enough so what is a servant? I think we all know a servant is a person who is devoted to another to serve. It can also be to serve a Cause, or creed, [doctrine, statement of faith, or country]. Now put them together, here's space for you to write your thoughts of what a bondservant is.

James firsts addresses trials. Now isn't that something? Right off the mark, he talks about what is in a person's life no matter how seasoned you are in Christ Jesus! Myself, I was going to God's house and living among churchgoers my entire life. Do I have trials? Of course! I am a bondservant of God and Jesus Christ therefore I will not be exempt from trials. God's word tells us we will have trials and/or temptation. I find it very encouraging to read James. Look at it closely.

*Verses 2 through 8: *"My brethren, count it all joy when you fall into various trials, 3. knowing that the testing of your faith produces patience. 4. But let patience have its perfect work, that you may be perfect and complete, lacking nothing. 5. If any of you lacks wisdom, let him ask of God, who gives* *to all liberally and without reproach, and it will be given to him. 6. But let him ask in faith, with no doubting, for he who doubts is like a wave of the sea driven and tossed by the wind. 7. For let not that man suppose that he will receive anything from the Lord; 8. he is a double-minded man , unstable in all his ways".* James is addressing how to look or perceive our trials- *count it all joy!* The living Bible says *'then be happy'* What happy in trials? Is he crazy? No, because we don't focus on the trial, but what the trial is doing within us. As you may notice there is a comma after the word trials, it is *verse three that tells us what and where our joy really is. Being joyful or happy **in a trial** is a **choice** not an **emotion**; therefore, the outcome is to grow in our faith, which produces patience. "Oh, you're saying, no wonder I'm going through so many trials, I've been praying for patience!" Could be, or are they because you're out of step with godly principles and He is trying like everything to get your attention? [That's usually me!].

*Verse four, *"but let patience have its perfect work, that you may be perfect and complete, lacking nothing".* This perfect means fully developed, or mature in your walk with Christ Jesus. Your walk will not be an emotional roller coaster, with highs and lows or sharp turns. But instead a steady upward walk. You may feel as if you're dodging a few potholes now and then, but I can testify it's more of a reminder not to let go of Jesus' hand. We lack nothing when we are holding the hand of Jesus Christ. He is the one that makes us complete, not ourselves. It is our choice to place our hand in His or not, but it is Jesus that makes us complete. He is the one that completes us when in a trial.

*Verse five, *"if any of you lacks wisdom, let him ask of God, who gives to all liberally and without* ***reproach****, and it will be given to him.* This wisdom James is talking of here is not mental power- remember, James is talking about facts of Christ and walking with Him. Therefore it is wisdom of the spirit-person, which again, puts it in our court to choose and ask for it. I love the words **liberal**, and **without reproach**! God is generous! When our sins are gone He doesn't give or deliver us from the evil one on the basis of **how** we behave, He no longer sees us as kids that tease, torment, or make fun of others, but as redeemed and growing followers of Him. –We need to thank God for that! Therefore, He will not hold anything against us from our past. He will not remind us of our unworthiness, or failures. Hallelujah for the blood that covers our sins! Read Psalm 103:12 and write it in the space provided here.

How far are our sins removed? How far can you walk east without going west? Or west until you're headed east? Meditate on this instead of that wild rock n roll music, the next party, the latest fashions—or boyfriends. It will get you farther in your walk with God, which is for eternity. Ok, I'll stop preaching and get back on track.

*Verse six, *"but let him ask in faith, with no doubting, for he who doubts is like a wave of the sea driven and tossed by the wind."*

Now that is **too much,** you say? So here's a question, can you have faith and doubting? It's like night or day, peas or cantaloupe total opposites! I looked in my thesaurus and the antonym for faith is – yep, doubt! And get this, the antonym for doubt was faith- or trusting! Now how about those apples—or carrots—so from what James is saying if you don't have faith, don't ask because you'll not receive it, **if you doubt.** Don't get discouraged, keep reading as all these verses are connected/related in meaning. *Verse seven, *"for let not that man suppose that he will receive* ***anything*** *from* the Lord; and *Verse eight is connected, "he is a **double-minded** man**, unstable in all his *ways."*** I told you James is very simple in his words and how he is frank, to the point didn't I? Do you want to know more who you are in Christ? Then take a good look at what a double-minded person is. You will decide for yourself if that is you, and what to do if it is. When doing research I found in every dictionary, thesaurus or other helps that one who is **double-minded** cannot make up their mind. They vacillate or change with circumstances, or because of others' influences. They are like up and down, opposite, one time they believe, then if the answer doesn't come when they expect it to, they give up hope in Him – forgetting God wears no watch, and hangs no calendars. For with God a day is like a thousand years, and a thousand years as one day! He is God! See 2 Peter 3:8 Let's take a break here, run through in our thoughts how trials and believing effect you, **who you are**! There is space below for you to jot your thoughts down; this will help you determine where you are **now** with God. Do you rejoice during a trial? Not the trial itself but that God is growing you up in Him? Put your thoughts here.

(a). Are you asking God when you lack **wisdom for your spirit life**?

(b). What kind of wisdom are you asking for? Is it for dealing with siblings, a job, certain task, or relationship that maybe going bad? Does it include your relationship with God? When you ask, is it in total, one hundred percent faith? Remember, if it is 99.9% it's not total faith. I want you to know this is something that will grow as you do in your faith and trust in the Lord. Will you waver if it doesn't take place immediately, in a day, month, year, or how about 20 or 40 years? You may be saying 'but I don't have that many years left', God knows that too --- do you believe that? Is what you're asking for really of Him? Remember, James here is talking about spiritual understanding. The purpose of the trial, to grow in your knowledge and relationship with Jesus Christ. His plan in you, not a contract you have in mind and present to Him, but allowing Him to live in you.

*Verses 9 through 11 James addresses *rich* and *poor.* It use to seem odd to me that James inserted this subject in such a few verses and right in the middle of talking about trials and temptations. However, I know **all** scripture is God anointed and it has a purpose being here at this spot in the Word. Lets look closer at what is being told us, to get a better perspective or view of who we are in Christ Jesus.

*** From the Living Bible Verses 9-11*"A Christian who doesn't amount to much in this world should be glad, for he is great in the Lord's sight. But a rich man should be glad that his riches mean* ***nothing*** *to the Lord, for he will soon be gone, like a flower that has lost its beauty and fades away, withered—killed by the scorching summer sun. so it is with rich men. They will soon die and leave behind all their busy activities."* What can test our faith the most? Think about it,---- m-o-n-e-y! If you can't pay bills, or go have fun with your friends, do you feel inadequate as a Christian as well as a person? So **you're basing your walk** with Christ Jesus with **how much dough/cash** you have in your account or pocket! What does the verse above say? Use the space provided to write out those thoughts.

It grows my spirit knowing my bank account has nothing to do with my walk with Christ Jesus! Yes, there are times when I truly wished and even prayed God would bless me so I didn't need to live in a single wide old trailer that the sewer smell penetrates my living space every winter! But does that hinder my growing with Jesus? No! God forbid! He has shown me many times how He takes care of me in spite of the putrid odor. He is providing my electricity so I can do my writing, which I know He has called me to do, so when personal bank account says NO way, my spirit can gratefully say yes, Yahweh! Pronounced, Yah way- meaning in Hebrew the LORD –I AM. Regardless of rich or poor, or in between, my walk with God is not, based or rooted upon my bank statement or balance!

Lets keep moving on to *Verses 12-18 **how** to keep loving God while we are under trials. Praise God, He doesn't keep us hanging but tells us **how** to deal with this circumstance.*12. *"Blessed is the man who endures temptation; for when he has been approved, he will receive the crown of life which the Lord has promised to those who love Him. 13. Let no one say when he is tempted, "I am tempted by God" for God cannot be tempted by* *evil, nor does He Himself tempt anyone. 14. But each one is tempted when he is drawn away by his own desires and enticed. 15. then, when desire has conceived, it gives birth to sin; and sin when it is full-grown, brings forth death. 16. Do not be deceived, my beloved brethren. 17. Every good gift and every perfect gift is from above, and comes down from the Father of lights, with whom there is no variation or shadow of turning. 18. Of His own will He brought us forth by the word of truth, that we might be a kind of firstfruits of His creatures.* It's great how James starts the discussion of being under trials and temptations. He starts off on a positive note. "blessed'—more than happy— have you ever experienced that feeling of accomplishment when you have performed above duty or what someone is wanting you to? Great! So you do know the jubilant emotion! Then we can keep going. Not only will you know that in your jubilant knower, you will be rewarded! I think most of us like that reward stuff. It's fun and exciting to receive an award for passing a test, or in this case a trial, or temptation. What does the "crown of life" mean here, you ask. From the Bible helps pre-mentioned, it is not talking about the life in heaven to come, but in fact a good life here on earth. When I really meditated and talked to the Holy Spirit what this means, it makes sense it is for the here and now, because when you're completely in the right you feel that abundance of living! I like to think of it as 'squeaky clean spirit'. You don't need to be concerned if you're telling people the same thing or story. If it is a fact, it is factual the whole truth and nothing else. Wow again huh? It connects the double-minded person in verse 8 wavering in all directions. So let us walk in the letter of the Word—God's Word and receive that jubilant blessed sensation, praising God He has made it possible for us to do so. I have given you space to write **your own thoughts and meditation** here. Not what others have said to you.

When I'm tempted I need to examine my walk. Are you asking why? Because it says so plainly, **God cannot be tempted**, therefore **He will not tempt anyone**! How simple and easy is that? Even a child can comprehend **cannot** and **will not**. Nothing but good, comes to us **from above**, all else is either of our own desires, be them selfish, which most of the time it stems from, or drawn away, like James says, to do things our way not God's way. I call this flying under the radar of godliness. It's not so bad to speed, or take your siblings' trinket—or how about that little untruth, some call 'white lie'? It stems from self, pride, and enticements – like a magnet, being drawn to something, -- just don't tell the **whole** truth, that way you may not get into trouble with the one in authority; be it parent, boss, the law, or whomever you're answering to at that particular time in your life. Take a firm look at this, because most of us go **through** and I mean **through** a stage where we either **stretch the truth**, [a lie] or **don't tell it like it really is** [a lie]. Most temptations begin with "but I didn't do it!" when in fact you did by causing the problem. You may not have personally thrown the ball, but you had someone else throw it. Get the meaning of what is being said here? Good, because James is not talking about the times God allows trials like for Job, but James is making it plain that these trials and temptations are **of our own doings**. Being drawn by our evil desires, when sin entered this world we all were handed a bad rap—sin—and sinning. But praise God we can be delivered when we lay down our will or self and ask Jesus to be our Savior. In this particular passage of God's word, it is telling us that in God's holiness He is above **all** evil, or sin. Since He is above that form of activity, He cannot delegate these actions of sinning to us. Why? Because it would be below **whom** He is! **He** didn't sin**, man** he created did. Verse fifteen can or could be very scary! Read it again, what does it say? *"When **desire** has conceived*", or taken root, it grows and grows, just as a baby in the womb. As a baby has allotted time then is born. Temptation is very much like that if we give it permission to linger in our desires, then it gives birth to sin! So, the temptation is **first a desire,** it moves from **a wish** to a **craving**, deep desire, more than a simple **thought!** When and if becomes an **action,** the battle is over its set in motion! It becomes real by **doing something** active, participating in, or saying, going or doing what is not or should not be. How do you think a shoplifter becomes a shoplifter? They **see,** they **desire,** they **do**. Usually it starts out with small items, then because they didn't get caught their confidence increases and so does the size of the items they steal. More realistically speaking, most kids begin their life by telling lies. If they are not corrected and taught ***not*** to lie as they age, so do the "I didn't do that, honest", or "I wasn't even there!" Then before long, it becomes a habit or known to God as a *stronghold*. What is a stronghold? Something you do **without** knowing you're doing it because it is a habit. Anything that has a **firm grip** on your lifestyle, **what** you say and **how** you say it is a stronghold, because **where** your **desires** are your heart and thoughts will be too. Here are a few scriptures that may help you understand this a little more. Jeremiah 16:19a in only the first seven words--- *"O LORD **my strength** and my fortress."* The word strength here means strong, power, security, and that is the way a stronghold operates. Where is your strength? Where is your power? Who is your security? Is it in yourself, doing what you want; or is it in God and what He wants? How often do you ask yourself, "what do you think about this_____, God?" You fill in the blank. Look up 2nd Corinthians 10:4 and discuss it with your teacher, mentor, or someone you trust to know the Word of God. Write your thoughts in this space

____

Sin is sin; God sees two colors, black, equaling sin, and white equaling purity. In the abstract world, black is the absence of white, just like darkness is the absence of light—but we'll not indulge any complications here, so black is black and white is white. Will your desires cause God to see a black mark on your life or will you not **yield** to the temptation? Remember, Jesus was tempted in every aspect of real earthly living, even as we are *Hebrews 4:15, yet without sinning. **In**

Verse 16 it tells us where our source of strength will come. Take the time to go back and read it for yourself. Then write it here:

Do you have this <u>firmly established</u> in your mind? It is **not Satan, nor God** that is tempting you, but **<u>your own</u>** desires! Check your strongholds, or habits. Write out your commitment to God in this space here—it will remind you of who you are serving. Don't forget to date it too

---

*Verses 17 and 18 are together read them again above. Does it say 'Every'? what is every? Just what I thought, all, complete. God is **all complete good!** no wiggle room! Because the tiniest bit of **bad** cannot exist in God! Well, shout it from the housetop! Hallelujah! God is not a schitzo! **WOW!** What a life of contentment we can have when we really absorb this nugget of truth! We don't need to **work at attaining** it because when we are **in Christ,** who is **The Truth, has attained** that for us! Praise God, hallelujah! Are you getting that jubilant feeling again? Me too! Then James goes on to say, *"not only every good gift but **every perfect** gift comes down form the Father of lights, with whom there is <u>no variation or shadow of turning.</u>"* Lets look at the word *variation* for a while. What is it? My good and faithful thesaurus came across once again, it is **inconsistency, discord, dispute, quarrel, or difference of opinion.** What a comfort to have **no variation** from the Father above! No shadows, all light! You can't have a shadow at high noon! The sun is direct, giving no shadows. God has no way of changing His mind, or not giving good because He **is all** good! Yeah, you can give another WOW!* 18, Regeneration, or being made new, in God through Christ Jesus who cleanses us from **all** unrighteousness 1st John 1:9 is God's most wonderful and **perfect** gift to us! Shouldn't this in itself tell us that God gives only good gifts? And to add "of His own will". He **chose** to reconcile us to himself through Jesus the Savior. Ephesians 1:13 don't forget, God knows all, sees all and loves all! God is good! Then comes the next question. Why? The last of that verse says *"that we might be a kind of firstfruits of His* ***creatures".*** So you're saying what is "firstfruits". It's like the first of a crop, or harvest, it was a pledge of a greater harvest to come. Just like the Christians in the Bible were the firstfruit of more Christians to come. The phrase "firstfruits of His creatures" is, we humans made in His image are redeemed at the confession of our mouth, so in the future when God rules the world all his creation or creatures will eventually know freedom of no evil curse. The ground was cursed and it brought forth weeds, what we see as bad, everything will be changed, the wolf will lay down with the lambs and not try to eat them. Gen.3:17b-19; 5:29b nature revived; Is. 11:6 *Verses 19 and 20 tell us the **qualities character or trait needed in trials.** *19 *"So then, my beloved brethren, let every man be* ***swift to hear, slow to speak, slow to wrath****: 20 for the wrath of man does not produce the righteousness of God.*

What do these two verses say to you? ____________________

What does it mean to be swift to hear? ____________________

Slow to speak ________________

Slow to wrath? _______________

What is wrath? ____________________

James gives us the answers to why these are not present in a Christian's walk, and are not of God. Put it in your own words what James is saying to you about the above three areas of ones walk with Jesus.

Now looking together at the word wrath. Find in your Bible Proverbs 15:18, lets discuss it and take it to heart by writing it in this space. if you're doing this as a self- study, think on it, then write your thoughts.

Does that mean we never get angry? I don't think so, for in Ephesians 4:26 it says, **"Be angry**, and ***do not sin***, <u>do not let the sun go down on your wrath"</u>... there is that word! **Wrath!** Angry is fuming, upset, the opposite of calm. **Wrath** is over and above angry when you lose it; not knowing what you're doing, outraged. Wrath is what causes fights to break out. (Most often also the root of arguments). Wrath is hurtful, unthinking, and tries to get the best **for itself**. Leads to selfishness. Has **no good**, does **no good**, in our walk/journey with God. [or any time.] Right now, take a good look at your life; does wrath have a place in your life? I am not talking about angry at the evil things that you see going on in the world, I am talking here of a **spirit of wrath**. Use this space to ask God to help you if you have that spirit of wrath, to break it and leave it at the cross.

*Verse 27 in Eph. 4, **"Nor give place to the devil".** The Greek word for **place** is **topos**, which means or emphasizes that a believer can give permission in their lives to satanic control. It makes it clear it is **the believer's responsibility** to control their tempers, not the devil creating it—we cannot easily blame the Devil for what **we** do with our emotions, or when **we** disobey God! Got it? Good, then the phrase, <u>'the Devil made me do it'</u> can be erased from your brain—**permanently** here and now lets travel on to

*Verse 20 and the righteousness of God.

Explain what **righteousness of God** is in this space provided. Compare it with the "discovery" listed below after you have written out your own explanation.

Break down the word **righteousness,** remove the suffix- **ness**—you have **righteous, which means:** moral, beyond good, just, upright, honorable, honest, respectable, everything that is the opposite of bad, or dishonorable. Now lets take it a step farther, and drop the "eousness"... we have **right** which means: correct, utterly true, accurate, exact, and precise. The opposite is wrong, inappropriate, and unsuitable. Go ahead, shout it out- WOW! Take a deep breath, and write out *Psalm 7: 9,10 and 17 in this space.

Doesn't that make verse twenty stand out that wrath will not produce, create or bring about **any** rightness of God within us as His? So what does?

We'll find more clues as we move on to *Verses 21 through 27 which tells us to be **doers not hearers only.** First we'll be talking about laying aside and what it means. *Verse 21 ***"Therefore lay aside*** *all filthiness and overflow of wickedness,* ***and receive with meekness the implanted word, which is able to save your souls."*** What is it to ***"lay aside"***—put your answer here

It's telling me it is in **our** ball-park, **our choice**, that when we have asked Jesus to be our Savior, the old nature of ourselves, our choices, should not be like they use to be. I love the paraphrased version in the Living Bible. It says; "So get **rid** of <u>all</u> that is wrong in ones life, **both inside and outside**". Could this outside not merely mean clean clothes? Could it mean what the world is doing (over-all body piercing, which is mutilating your temple of the Lord). Seeing/looking at porn, and going places such as movies that damage, not build up, your walk with God? Hanging out with questionable persons is just as bad. Ask yourself many times this question, "would God be welcomed in this ______________ place? You fill in the blank. We have **done away** with that person's selfish freewill. Instead, we have taken on the humility of Salvation for our soul! What a marvelous, miraculous choice we have made! Trade in the old self and be made completely new with a reward too—Salvation of our soul! How is this done? Coming to Jesus by faith accepting Jesus to be in us! Find and read John 1:12-13. When we receive something—what does that mean? Write it here.

____

Now lets look at the word **implant.** I'm sure you know it means to **place within, to insert something, to graph or be graphed** here it is God's Word! Yes, remember, **God cannot lie---** we can by faith, trust what He has told us in His Word.

Now I don't consider myself ancient, nor historic, but perhaps the forties and fifties were olden days, because I remember my father making a deal or contract with other farmers that rented property from him with merely a handshake! It was the latter part of his life when people asked him to loan them money do I recall him writing up a written agreement. No more did he loan with a **faith-trust** handshake. How sad in a way that he couldn't trust what the other person's intent was. But thank God, He can be trusted by faith **all** the time! It is God's **Word,** His "contract" of commitment to us. Now make that personal, what is God saying to **me**? Is there any 'filthiness' in **my** life?

That is a yes or no question, so which is it? **Circle** the correct answer… now define that "filthiness," it may be; bad language, unclean habits, whatever keeps you from growing in meekness and godliness. Write it here.

____

Again, just as we did before, blot it out by gluing or taping **red construction paper** over what you have committed to Jesus. You have just given it to God, don't dig it up it might be smelly for "old things are passed away, behold all things are made new."

2nd Corinthians 5:17. You're now walking in the Spirit, you have taken **<u>action</u>** to stop the nagging thoughts of whatever it was you **laid aside**. You now can denounce whatever it was whenever you're thoughts rise to that situation, circumstance, or habit. Whatever it was you wrote is **gone**! In this space write praise to God for making it possible to **lay aside** those strongholds.

*Verse 22 *"But be doers of the word, and not hearers only, deceiving yourselves."* Lets look and discuss the following scriptures in our Bible concerning how it is when we **deceive ourselves.**

Matthew 7:22 & 23 ________________________________

Luke 6:46-49 ______________________________________

Romans 2:13 _______________________________________

****23 "For if anyone is <u>a hearer</u> of the word and <u>not a doer</u>, he is like a man [person] observing his natural face in a mirror; 24 for he observes himself, goes away, and immediately forgets what kind of man [person] he/she was."*** After re-reading this passage, comparing different versions, and much prayer, I am seeing more clearly how important it is to be **a doer.** It is taking action, serving God. Going to church, or youth group, talking like a believer, using the scripture to prove a point, are all good, but yet not a doer. It's like having a glance in the mirror and forgetting what you saw. This "doer:" is * 'to experience a **transformation** in your life which brings about ministry or service to Him who saved you.' A doer is **obedience** to what God has asked you to do, say or go. Do you know what that may be? Write it here as a commitment between Him and you.

____

____

That doesn't mean it is in stone, you may hear Him saying something new later in your walk with Him. The important thing is to listen, pray, then obey! **25." But he who looks into the perfect law of liberty and continues in it and is not a forgetful hearer but a doer of the work, this one will be blessed in what he does."(Some translations put in "word" instead of "work")* Obedience equals blessings. It's a simple humble act for all God has provided for us. God's word is **freedom, not slavery**- it is **your choice** in which much joy and peace reign. It is a desire, or compulsion, something within our spirit that desires to do, and be.

*Verse *26 "If anyone among you thinks he is religious, and does not bridle his tongue but deceives his own heart, this one's religion is useless.* "What does this verse say to you? Write it here, ____________________

____

Find and read Psalm 34:12 –14. Notice the words: **keep, depart and seek**! They are all action words, something **we choose** to do. Remember when you're reading the Word to look for the action words. That is where life is! "An **uncontrolled tongue** and **a deceived heart** are companions of an **empty religion,** or **belief**. True Christ-likeness will issue practical living, expressed with **pure speech**, (no disgusting talk, swearing, bad jokes) **genuine love**, (sincere, real, not a sexual type but brotherly/sisterly type of love) and **wholesome** (moral, clean and honest) character (personality, disposition, and Soul) *Verse *27 "Pure and undefiled religion before God and the Father is this: to visit orphans* *and widows in their trouble, and to keep oneself unspotted from the world." (in some versions the word "unspotted" is " unpolluted")* Look up Matthew 5:8 in your Bible and notice the word blessed. It says happy, a condition in which congratulations are in order. Expressing the **special joys** and satisfaction granted the person who **experiences salvation**. The over powering jubilant emotion we talked about when we first began our journey in James. **Who is happy?**

Last but not least of all this **walking** Christian experience, is to ***'keep oneself unspotted or unpolluted from the world'.*** Discuss and write out what you consider **unspotted or unpolluted from the world** means in this space

I*n a nut shell:*

1. Be **unspotted** is to be **Un-**influenced, **UN**-soiled or **not** foul-mouthed, or having intentions such as **UN**-believers.
2. It is to have intense love and trust for and in God and His word that **all** the world and what is in it is not ruling us.
3. Nothing becomes more important to us than growing in God's love, extending it to those we live with, and associate with on a daily basis. Not preaching to them, but in our conduct and character. Following the Holy Spirit's leading and abiding or living in Christ. Romans 6:8-11 *"Now if we died with Christ, we believe that we shall also live with Him, knowing that Christ, having been raised from the dead, dies no more. Death no longer has dominion over Him. For the death that He died, He died to sin once for all; but the life that He lives, He lives to God, likewise you also, reckon yourselves to be dead indeed to sin, but alive to God* ***in Christ Jesus our Lord.***

How to grow from this chapter study:

A good way to stay cleansed is to **wash your Spirit and Soul** after being out among those who do not know Christ in the way you do. Here is a sample of how to wash your spirit:** **I declare in the name of Jesus that I'm cleansed of any and all of the defilements I may have walked through today. Every vile, dirty or unclean thing that has assaulted my eyes, ears, and mind is wiped away and forbidden to find a place in my soul or spirit. Every unsettling or upsetting thing is conquered by the peace of Jesus that is given to me and I'm covered and protected by the blood of Jesus that is applied to my Spirit, soul and body and all my gates by the power of the Holy Spirit who lives in me. I bless myself with peace; I bless myself with rest; I bless myself with revelation in the knowledge of Jesus Christ and the wisdom that He is to me. I declare that I am hidden with Christ in God Almighty who is my refuge. In Jesus Holy Name amen!**

Cross references for this chapter:

Verse one: Acts 12:17, **Verse two**: Acts 5:41, 1st Peter 1:6 **Verse three:** Rom 5:3-5, **Verse five**: 1st Kings 3:9; Proverbs 2:3-6; Matt 7:7 Jer 29:12, **Verse six:** Mark 11:23-24; Acts 10:10, **Verse eight:** James 4:8, **Verse ten**: Job 14:2, **Verse twelve**: Job 5:17;Luke 6:22; Heb 10:36, 1st Peter 3:14; 4:14; 1st Cor 9:25, Mat 10:22 **Verse fifteen:** Job 15:35, Ps 7:14; Isa 59:4; Rom 5:12, **Verse seventeen:** John 3:27; Num 23:19, **Verse eighteen**: John 1:13; 2nd Cor 6:7; 1st Thess 2:13; 2nd Tim 2:15; Eph 1:12-13; Heb 12:23; Rev 14:4, **Verse nineteen**: Prov 10:19; 17:27; 14:17; 16:32; Ecc 7:9 **Verse twenty-one:** Col 3:8; Acts 13:26, **Verse twenty-two:** Matt 7:21-28; Luke 6:46-49; Rom 2:13**, Verse twenty-five:** John 8:32, Rom 8:2; 2nd Cor 3:17; Gal 2:4; Gal 6:2; 1st Pet 2:16; John 16:17 **Verse twenty-six:** Ps 34:13, **Verse twenty-seven:** Mat 25:34-36; Isa 1:17; Rom 12:2

Chapter Two

In this second chapter we will look at the first thirteen verses which shows that an **empty religion** will demonstrate partiality/prejudice based on ones own assumptions stemming from race, riches, or education.

Lets get digging!

**Verse one "My brethren, do not hold the faith of our Lord Jesus Christ, the Lord of glory, with partiality".* [Brethren identifies fellow believers]. *2 For if there should come into your assembly a man with gold rings, in fine apparel, and there should also come in a poor man in filthy clothes, 3 and you pay attention to the one wearing the fine clothes and say to him 'You sit here in a good place' and say to the poor man, 'you stand there' or, 'Sit here at my footstool,' 4 have you not shown partiality among yourselves, and become judges with evil thoughts?"*

Wow! James doesn't hold back any punches, does he? When was the last time a person dressed in the finest of threads or a person, dirty or filthy entered your church?

Below is a story of what happened in my church-if you don't need to read this for yourself, allow your teacher/leader to read it to you while you close your eyes to block out any distraction. If you do need to read it yourself, pause and meditate on the correlation of what the scripture and story have in common. Notice the action.

Envision this happening; your head turns as the door opens and in walks your favorite Christian singer, [*pause one second]* oh, taking a closer or second look, guess it's not that person after all! Whew, your heart slows down a fraction and you take a deep breath. However they certainly remind you of her/him! They're modestly dressed, yet look like they just stepped out of the *vogue* catalog. You know, hair in place and very stylish, clothing all pressed and tidy, teeth brushed and breath smelling like cool mint in and open field. [*Pause again for a second]* Oh, did I mention, they wore a big smile and had that magnetic personality? Well, consider that too…[Pause} NOW: Right behind that gorgeous person who smelt so yummy entered a person **not** so stylish. She/he looks tired from the lack of good rest, hair is messed up because she/he had no comb to remove the snarls, and grim. Was more than *double-layered* with clothing. Smelled like their dog, which kept them warm at night, teeth that hadn't been brushed in who knows how long, and you know their breath will smell like garbage, after all that's where she/he ate last! Getting the picture? My fellowship is located on the outskirts of town and have seen a few of the latter described! YES, honest! I was so happy of how the men in the church welcomed that person, you know, by shaking his hand—though it was not the cleanest looking hand they'd seen that morning. I made the choice to talk to him too. Come to find out he loves God with all his heart and is a born again believer! Which would you rather sit beside? Which would God want you to sit with? Discuss or think on this with an *honest* heart*! God knows before you speak or write it what you were thinking as the paragraphs were being read to you--- or you read them.*

Because the rich and poor are among us, what and how do we choose to treat them? Do we flatter, or cater, to the rich, while on the other hand we shun or discriminate the poor? Remember, action speaks louder than words, and how we respond will determine the true value of our partiality in such cases. This is not saying to give a handout to the ones holding signs as you come off the freeway/turnpikes, but the ones entering your place of fellowship! Even then allow the Holy Spirit to direct your response. Yes, there are those who take advantage of a church to get whatever they can, eventually becoming more and more dependant upon others and never working for themselves. As a kid I was shy and very naive so in high school, which did, I gravitate to? The "under-dog" those that had less money, yes they were clean! I learned these kids were not so "odd" as some of the kids thought. Always, and I say again, **always** allow the Holy Spirit to guide you to your friends! Just because you're nice to someone doesn't mean you will be lifetime buddies, or hang with them daily. Let's continue seeing what God says about the poor in verses five to ten.

*Verse 5. "*Listen, my beloved brethren; has God not chosen the poor of this world to be rich in faith and heirs of the kingdom, which He promised to those who love Him? 6 But you have dishonored the poor man. 7 Do not the rich oppress you and drag you into the courts? 8 If you really fulfill royal law according to the Scripture, 'You shall love your neighbor as yourself' you do well; 9 but if you* ***show partiality****, you commit sin, and are convicted by the law as transgressors. 10 For whoever shall keep the whole law, and yet stumble in one point, he is guilty of all."*

Most often the poor will have the greater faith, because they feel they don't have much knowledge. Not all rich people have turned their back on God but in this illustration, God is referring to us Christians choosing to be nice, hospitable and showing honor to the rich, when He, God, shows mercy, love, grace, blessings, and benefits of His salvation to ALL! Rich and poor! Human value cannot be equaled with race, wealth, social standing, or educational level to God! All, everybody, is important, or valuable to God, and to say that a race, group, or individual in dirty/shabby clothes is not important **by our behavior towards them**, is sin! Stop! Did you say SIN? No, but God did! That's right, read on, it says 'to him it is **s I n** – no, I didn't do a boo-boo—notice that capital I? Yep, right smack in the middle is **I** [or me for proper English]. It usually is ourselves in the center when we sin. In this case it definitely is the root or center because our behavior is superior to whomever it is that has filthy rags—getting the picture? Good! Lets keep tracking on this journey.

James, full of the Spirit was passing on God's value on human life. **All** human life! Not just the rich, well educated, or those offering something to this world in their term of what that means, but by God's standard, read Psalm 139:13-18. What did it say? What does it say to you?

If you said that God saw us and knitted our body together intricately, you are correct! Each and every one comes into this world the same way, born of a woman, bare bottomed and crying! Yes, that's right! Rich or poor, educated or not, genius or average, president or servant, preacher or toilet scrubber, the list is long, we all made our entry into this world the same equal way—in a body with a Spirit and soul! Praise God, He did a magnificent job and whom do we think we are that we have permission to discriminate? If you have any thoughts or comments please journal them here, Why? Because Jeremiah 30:2 says, " *Thus speaks the LORD God of Israel, saying:"* *'Write in a book for* **yourself** *all the words that I have spoken to you"* Now isn't that reason enough? I think so.

I pray each reader has found favor with God and themselves on this issue of prejudice and or favoritism for it is time to travel on to the "trail" of faith without works is dead.

Verse 11 *"For He who said, 'Do not commit adultery', also said, 'Do not murder,' now if you don't commit adultery, but do murder, you have become a transgressor of the law. 12 So speak and so do as those who will be judged by the law of liberty. 13 For judgment is without mercy to the one who has shown no mercy. Mercy triumphs over judgment".* In the resource from the Spirit Life Bible this is explained as follows:* James does not teach that to commit **one sin**, such as **murder** or **adultery**, is to be

guilty of **every other individual sin** listed in the law. He views the law as an expression of **God's will**, which is an unbroken or unfragmented whole. So by breaking **any part of the law** constitutes to disregarding God's will or rebelling **against God.**

Faith Without Works Is Dead:

*Verse 14-26 "*what does it profit, my brethren, if someone says he has faith but does not have works? Can faith save him? 15 If a brother or sister is naked and destitute of daily food, 16 and one of you says to them 'Depart in peace, be warmed and filled,' but you do not give them the things which are needed for the body, what does that profit? 17. Thus also faith by itself, if it does not have works, is dead. 18 But someone will say 'You have faith, and I have works.' Show me your faith without your works, and I will show you my faith by my works. 19 You believe that there is one God. You do well.* <u>Even the demons believe—and tremble!</u> *20 But do you want to know, o foolish man, that faith without works is dead? 21 Was not Abraham our father justified by works when he offered Isaac his son on the alter? 22 Do you see that faith and* ***working together*** *with his works, and by works faith was made perfect? 23 And the Scripture was fulfilled which says, '****Abraham believed God, and it was accounted to him for righteousness.'*** *And he was called the friend of God. 24 You see then that a man is justified by works, and not by faith only. 25 Likewise, was not Rahab the harlot also justified by works when she received the messengers and sent them out another way? 26 For as the body without the spirit is dead, so faith without works is dead also."* Wow! Take a deep breath and stretch out your arms--- if you want to stand do so, because there is a lot of good discoveries in this Scripture! What is "work"—yep, write it down how you see it. ________________________________.

What is "faith" again, write your definition here. ______________

____

Now read Ephesians 2:8-10 in order to refer back to what has been said, write it down in this space. You can put it in your own wording if you wish.

Did you define the difference in the two words **"work"** and **"faith"** according to God's definition or is it yours? The Holy Spirit ministers to me that both works and faith walk side by side just as friends do. This works that James is talking about is **not** earning your way to heaven! For the scripture above proves that concept or idea. James is saying you can't have faith **without doing** something, just as Jesus did in Matthew 25:40. It's **showing** the world around us we are saved. However, don't think for a moment you can only do good or thoughtful things—just as Jesus said in Matthew "in as much as **you did** it to one of **the least** of these My brethren, you **did it unto me**." Yep! Just like Jesus, James is saying, "the faith you **have** is the faith you **show."** Have you ever been in need and someone showed you God's love by helping you? Perhaps you needed an article of clothing, food, or even housing, and someone stretched his or her bucks, and paid for you to have what you need? Do you feel you would have faith to **do** for someone God tells you to? No, it doesn't always involve money, most often it will be **your time!** However lets say you only have fifty dollars and God knows you have a bill or need that will take all but ten of it but tells you to give the whole fifty to that person. Now where is your faith? Where is your works? That is exactly what happened to me a long time ago when I had two children to support. What did I do? I remembered this passage and told God "okay, I'll do it!" I wasn't really surprised when that person told me thank you and it was exactly what he needed! Two days later and only a week before my bill came due I received a blessing from somebody else. It more than covered my bill! Praise God! It still brings tears to my eyes to know how much God loves each and every one of us! I told you this testimony to show you Christianity is an action word, not passive. It is obedience with faith, and love for God as well as our fellow traveler. Is not inactive but active! Therefore, when you walk by faith you'll be willing to do something too. I love the drastic contrasts God had James recall for us from the Old Testament! Abraham and Rahab! Did you notice the two drastic differences that these two people were? Abraham known for his righteous living and Rahab known as a harlot or prostitute! God did this to show us that he is not a respecter of persons; He will use those who trust in Him and are obedient to doing what he requires. It is also showing both social and moral scale in which God will move which brings justification to all. How did verse 19 challenge you? I know it makes me want to tell people that say they believe – "Big Deal! So do the demons and their response is Trembling in Fear of a Holy God!" This is how the Living Bible puts it: "Are there still some among you who hold that 'only believing' is enough? Believing in one God? Well, remember that the demons believe this too--- so strongly that they tremble in terror! Fool! When will you ever learn that 'believing' is useless **without doing** what God wants you to? Faith that does not result in good deeds is not real faith" Do you know someone that is like that? They have said they believe, however, their actions say quite the opposite? If so pray God will open their spiritual eyes that they might repent and be obedient to Him. Last verse for this section and chapter read it again; "just as the Body is dead without a Spirit;" **wow**, no life at all! We are made in the **image** of God! He **breathed His Spirit** into our form, therefore, without His Spirit within us our body would be dead! That is the exact picture James is saying of having faith in God and **doing** His work.

In a nutshell

1. Be aware of favoritism or partiality and remember why not to do so. It's called S-I-N! James says in chapter four verse seventeen, "to **know** to do right and not doing it is sin!" yep, we will be touching this again!

2. By breaking one you are guilty of all the law, just as if when you get a ticket and you are before the judge, he says you are a law-breaker. Why? You only broke the speed limit, not stole or murdered! Yet you have now a title, "law-breaker" you broke the speed! Just as a little girl once said, "I only told a little lie, I didn't break all the commandments, only cracked them!"
3. There is perfect harmony with works and deeds! Why? When you do works only, your aim is getting to heaven with good works. Put them together,*it is **vertical faith** in God and **horizontal works** to a needy world. This makes a +, Faith is both spiritual and practical.

How to grow from this chapter study:

1. Take notes, mentally or by writing them down in a journal, what you're doing each day as you do good deeds. [do they glorify God or those watching]?
2. Do you show partiality to the well-dressed or social class of kids, or people your age?
3. Always remember, God extends grace to you, will you extend grace to others? [Grace will refrain from passing judgment to the offending person when they could pursue or press charges.]

Cross references for chapter two.

Verse one: Acts 7:2, 1st Cor.2: 8, Lev. 19:15 --- **Verse five:** Job 34:19, John 7:48, 1st Cor. 1:27, Luke 12:21, 1st Tim. 6:18, Ex. 20:6 **Verse six:** 1st Cor. 11:22, Acts 13:50 **Verse seven**: Acts. 11:26, 1st Peter 4:16 **Verse eight:** Lev. 19:15 **Verse ten**: Gal. 3:10 **Verse thirteen**: Job 22:6, Rom. 12:8 **Verse fourteen:** Matt. 7:21-23, 26:21, 28:32, **Verse fifteen**: Luke 3:11**, Verse eighteen**: Col. 1:6, 1st Thess.1: 3, Heb. 6:10, **Verse twenty-one**: Gen.22: 9,10,12,16-18 **Verse twenty-two**: John 6:29, Heb. 11:17 1st John 2:5 **Verse twenty-three**: Gen. 15:6, Rom. 4:3,2nd Chron.20: 7 **Verse twenty-five**: Heb. 11:31

Chapter Three

Chapter three in James gives more than half his attention to one particular subject. **The tongue**! Why would that be? It's only a small part of the body, right? What harm could the tongue do? Lets look at this muscle or organ and see what all it does. It aids in the digestion of food, contains perception of taste, and oh, yes, we humans couldn't pronounce our words! In my study of the tongue I realized how many things have a tongue! Of course all animals, insects and even some fish Then there are <u>things</u> like the flap on a shoe, the clapper of a bell, the pin of a buckle, the pole of a wagon, the projecting tension of a tongue-and-groove joint, in machines a projecting flange, rib, the vibrating end of the reed in a wind instrument, and the list could go on, and on—but I feel you're getting the idea. How different **our** tongue than all these listed here! No wonder God felt it was very important for James to address this issue. Out of all these, the human tongue can pronounce and utter words in speech so as to communicate with one another! It also gives us **taste!** What an amazingly important part of our body; wouldn't you agree? The first thing I thought of was the verse in Psalm 34:8 where it says "O' taste and see that the Lord is good"! Wow, not only can we know God is in us, but we can actually taste His goodness! That is if the tongue is under what James is talking about. So are you ready to get digging for nuggets on the tongue?

Let's get digging!

The Untamed Tongue

Verse 1: "My brethren, let not many of you become teachers, knowing that we shall receive a stricter judgment."* Let's take a look at what James is saying in this because it sounds like you should not seek or desire to be a teacher. What happens to teachers/preachers of the Word of God? They are most often unfairly criticized. Leaders in the Kingdom of God are judged not so much by what they **accomplish as by the **character** they reveal—**who** they **are** before what **they do**. This high standard applies not so much to the leader's achievements as to the condition of his or her heart and spirit. It is possible to have a grand performance without love! However, if the leader's heart is right and godly his or her behavior will always manifest it! Godliness or God-likeness! Looking farther into this matter the verse says without saying it specifically. Teachers are responsible for those they are teaching or influencing. Mat. 23:1-10 in which Jesus is warning against a prideful seeking of public praise, exemplified by the desire for places of prominence and titles signifying superiority. It is the **attitude** behind the **seeking if** such recognition that Jesus condemns. As believers, we are equal and owe our reverence to Christ alone. This leadership will be proven. It will not contain bad or questionable language. A buzzer sound will not go off in your Spirit when they're talking, joking, or just goofing off with you. They will not teach that it's okay to go against God's Parental Principles, as established in the Bible. They will only attend Godly movies. Not loiter in any place, but be there to witness for Jesus. A good Godly leader will be so **in love** with the **value of people** that he will be fully or always aware of his/her witness or testimony as not to make anyone stumble in their personal life by hanging with unruly individuals, doing questionable things and **using their tongue** in anyway to destroy godly values! Rest assuredly, God is the judge of the heart! It is He that we all shall answer to. Teacher or student.

Verse 2. "For we all stumble in many things. If anyone does not stumble in word, he is a* ***perfect* *man, able also to bridle the whole body."* Perfect here refers to that which has reached an end that is finished, complete, perfect. When applied to persons, it signifies complete soundness, and includes the idea of being whole. More particularly, when applied to believers it stands for **maturity** and **self control**.

Verse 3- 4. "Indeed, we put bits in horses' mouths that they may obey us, and we turn their whole body. 4. Look also at ships: although they are so large and are driven by fierce winds, a very small rudder turns them wherever the captain desires".* Our ships today are generated by engines not strong winds but still contain a rudder. How interesting to me that this is an example of our tongue! Key word here is **discipline. Ask yourself if you are disciplining your thoughts and actions. This discipline is saying **no** to yourself when in desire you want to do what you know you shouldn't be doing. It is **not** injuring yourself with cutting, or pinching or being abusive to your flesh, but a right spirit before God who gives you the strength to say **no!**

*Verse 5-6. *"Even so* ***the tongue*** *is a little member and boasts great things. See how a forest a little fire kindles! 6. and the tongue is a fire, a world of iniquity. The tongue is so set among our members that it defiles the whole body, and sets on fire the course of nature; and it is set on fire by hell"* Can't you just see this huge forest fire burning? It took only one small spark, the right temperature and small breeze to get it going! That's like our tongue when and if we whisper one bad or negative word to somebody else. It may be about yourself, but simply the right **temper**ature a breeze of jealousy or resentment, and the fire starts! You know what I'm talking about, correct? We call it spreading rumors. It is more than difficult to put out a rumor, even as it is a forest fire. We see huge fires on TV each summer. How much better it would have been had that spark never been left to ignite or that whispered negative word about someone to be spread! In verse seven James is saying some very important things. Let's read on.

Verses 7- 12. "For every kind of beast and bird, of reptile and creature of the sea, is tamed and has been tamed by mankind. 8. But* ***no* *man can tame the tongue. It is an unruly evil, full of deadly poison. 9. With it we bless our God and Father, and with it we curse men, who have been made in the similitude [likeness] of God. 10. Out of the same mouth proceed blessing and cursing. My brethren, these things ought not to be so. 11. Does a spring send forth fresh water and bitter from the same opening? 12. Can a fig tree, my brethren, bear olives, or a grapevine bear figs? Thus no spring yields both salt* *water and fresh.*" All I can say is "how interesting!" Isn't that interesting how the Word of God says that mankind can and has mastered taming all sorts of critters, but we cannot **tame the little tongue** in our mouth! Then who or what can tame the tongue? Only God can! We need saved from our own sinful body member the tongue! Slander or rumors or whatever you call it are all ungodly and **not** for the **true** Christian! These are learned one day at a time! Setting goals with God and walking the path of **obedience**! In Psalm 140:3 David is praying to God to deliver him from the evil men who were **slandering** him with their **tongues**. He called it "sharpening their tongues like a serpent". Did you notice before Christ came they too had a problem with their tongue? Paul was slandered in the New Testament, as was Jesus, how much more do you and I lay victim to it too. Or will we be the one **guilty** of slander? What comes from your mouth on a daily basis? Would you be brave enough to write some of it here and then surrender [give it entirely] to God [your tongue]? Good, I presume you are ready to have only clear, fresh, living and energizing water [language] coming from your tongue so I will leave you space to do that here.

____

____

Think first, meditate, and make sure you are ready to be honest. Remember, God knows what you're thinking even if you write something else.

Heavenly and Demonic Wisdom. Could this be fresh water and bad water?

Let's get digging!

*Verses 13 –18 "*Who is wise and understanding among you? Let him show by good conduct that his works are done in the meekness of wisdom. 14 But if you have bitter envy and self-seeking in your hearts, do not boast and lie against the truth. 15 This wisdom does not descend from above, but* *is earthly,* ***sensual,*** *and demonic. 16 For where envy and self-seeking exist, confusion and every evil thing are there. 17 But the wisdom that is from above is first pure, then peaceable, gentle, willing to yield, full of mercy and good fruits, without partiality and without hypocrisy. 18 Now the fruit of righteousness is sown in peace by those who make peace".* For clarification of what Paul is saying I will give you the Paraphrased Living Bible version. *** 13 "If you are wise, live a life of steady goodness, so that only good deeds will pour forth. And if you don't brag about them, then you will be truly wise! 14 And by all means don't brag about being wise and good if you are bitter and jealous and selfish; that is the worst sort of lie. 15 For jealousy and selfishness is not God's kind of wisdom. Such things are earthly, unspiritual, inspired by the devil. 16 For wherever there is jealousy or selfish ambition, there will be disorder and every other kind of evil. 17 But the wisdom that comes from heaven is first of all pure and full of quiet gentleness. Then it is peace loving and courteous. It allows discussion and is willing to yield to others; it is full of mercy and good deeds. It is wholehearted and straightforward and sincere. 18 And those who are peacemakers will plant seeds of peace and reap a harvest of goodness." How plain is that? To make sure you get the difference between heavenly and demonic wisdom I have put two columns below to list the differences.

Demonic wisdom:	Heavenly Wisdom:

Which is the most appealing to you? ______________________. Will you put into practice immediately the heavenly wisdom? ______________________. [I presume this was your choice of the two columns above]. So, what is your plan to activate this? Write them here..

Look up (Old Testament) Zechariah 4:6b. How will you complete this heavenly wisdom? Make it personal ______________________ None of us can do any heavenly good without God's Holy Spirit alive and well **in** us. We have a free will to choose, however, it is God's Spirit **in us** that will give us the strength. Check it out in Philippians 4:13 and write it here to remind you of **where** your strength will come from **in** your walk with and **in** Christ Jesus.

In a nut shell:

1. *James told those who desired to be teachers they need to* ***practice*** **what they teach** above all. **God's love** must be in a true teacher. My Papa always said, 'by **your words** you will be labeled'. How right on he was! He may be in heaven but his words are still alive **in** me. How blessed I am!
2. If a teacher is **motivated** by their **own selfish desires** there will be lies against the truth. It's for the purpose of saying "look at me" or "look at what I've done one".
3. Seek Heavenly Wisdom!

How to grow from this chapter study

I feel a need to transcribe a re-paraphrasing of 1st Corinthians 13 that God in His marvelous and gentle approach gave to me when I questioned within myself if I was really hearing Him calling me into this wonderful world of teaching. This is what He said that night.

Teachers

I am not a teacher because I obtain all the equipment, glue, scissors, and lesson manual. If I have all the construction paper, glitter, Bible, posters and activity units, and have **not** LOVE for my students, I'm no more than a supply center. Though I possess all knowledge of the lesson, Bible in hand and faithfully attend all meetings; but have not LOVE for the students, I'm like a well-prepared movie star.

Though my appearance is neat and well groomed with a smile to all I meet, but have **not** LOVE for the students, I'm like anyone walking out of a beauty salon having a good day. If I put my problems on hold and bear the problems of the students, and their parents' but have **no** LOVE, I'm only gathering data for my own interest. A teacher **will not** have a favorite, but **will have** LOVE for **all** students. A teacher **will remember** that where crayons, lesson activities, white-board, they shall burn, and the printed page will fade, but the <u>student reached by LOVE shall last forever.</u> A teacher **will not** seek the title as "teacher" for vain glory, but to the glory of God. A right relationship with God will be enough to surpass all criticism. A teacher **will know** that all success is a result of Gods LOVE.

Now abides preparation, supplies, and love, but the **greatest** of all **is LOVE**!

My dear, dear travelers on this growth journey, I love you so much yet I probably won't ever have the privilege of knowing you personally! My prayer is that you'll find strength in the Holy Spirit to **walk the talk** and **do all** to the glory of God **that He desires for you**! Walk in His LOVE!

Cross references for Chapter three:

Verse one: Matt 23:8, Rom. 2:21, 1st Tim. 1:7 **Verse two**: 1st Kings 8:46, Ps. 34:13, Matt. 12:34-37 the whole verse is talking of Maturity, as explained in the study. **Verse three**: 2nd Thess. 3:4 **Verse five**: Prov 12:18, 15:2 Ps. 12:3, 73:8 **Verse six**: Prov 16:27, Matt. 12:36, 15:11 &

18, **Verse eight**: Ps.140:3 **Verse nine**: Gen. 1:26, 5:1, 9:6 **Verse twelve**: Matt. 7:16-20 **Verse thirteen**: Gal. 6:4 **Verse fourteen**: Rom. 13:13, Rom. 2:17 **Verse fifteen**: Phil. 3:9 **Verse sixteen**: 1st Cor. 3:3 **Verse seventeen**: 1st Cor. 2:6,7, Rom. 12:9 **Verse eighteen**: Prov. 11:18

Chapter Four

Chapter four gives us an overview of worldliness and **godliness. Quarreling** and **wars,** where do they come from, or what is the root of them? I have always liked looking at words. Not what they mean necessarily, but how they are spelled. Like C-H-**I**-L-D,

S-**I**-N, P-R-**I**-D-E-notice the "I" is in the center. "**I**", unquestionably what a <u>child</u> thinks of. Repeatedly the first phrase that a child says without being taught is, "Mine"—who's first? "I"! Same with sin, we naturally came into sin when we were born in this world, however we can be delivered from it by receiving Jesus Christ into our life. After that we choose to sin, why? Look at the middle letter again. "I"! We studied that in the first part of James. Tempted of our own self, or selfish desires. So we're thinking of I. You've seen cartoons with an angel on one shoulder and the devil on the other shoulder. Should I do this or that; saying something before thinking it through, or behaving like God wants me to, or what "I" want. Continually warring. If not with yourself it's with someone else and what they are doing against what you think, again the "I" thinking. The war begins within us! On the opposing of **I** is **U** take the word A-D-**<u>U</u>**-L-T, what is the opposite of **I**? In this case it is **U** so lets change the **I** in sin to **U** and the result is S-**<u>U</u>**-N, and when we think or see the sun we think of light, warmth, and most of us love the sun. Remember **God's light** to the world is **His SON**. I'm praying you'll see the correlation and find it interesting to compare the "**I**"-z in your life with the "**U**"- z? Who was God thinking of when He sent his son? **U** of course! You can't spell **you** without the **U**, no more than you can spell **Jesus, crucified** and **resurrection** without the **U!**

I'm glad all those words include **U** ---- Aren't you? I get so carried away sometimes with the intricate way our language in one word, carries a complete message in itself. For instance I mentioned the word P-R-**I**-D-E, notice it carries that "**I**" in the center! How self-involved it even sounds! Say these words slowly, out loud and together if doing this as a group journey: sin, child, and pride a few times! Now do the same with these words: Jesus, crucified, resurrection and adult! With those thoughts in your mind, are you ready to discover new nuggets? The first is on pride, then how to free oneself of this worldliness.

Let's get digging!

Pride promotes strife

Verses 1-6 "Where do wars and fights come from among you? Do they not come <u>***from your desires***</u> <u>*for pleasure*</u> *that war in your members? [Mind, or soul-person] 2 You lust and do not have. You murder and covet and cannot obtain. You fight and war. Yet you do not have because you do not ask. "You ask and do not receive, because you ask amiss, that you may spend it on your pleasures."* Here we are looking at **motive,** the motive for what we-or I want. My father instructed his six children to always check our **motive** for what we ask for or why we desired to do something, then come to him and make our request known to him. How much more important is it to do that with our heavenly Father? Verse **4 "Adulterers and adulteresses*!" These titles are referring to Old Testament symbolic terms for those who break their vows to love and serve God. Instead they follow idols. An idol can be **anything** that makes God second in our life. The very next sentence proves that point! *Verse 4b *"Do you not know that friendship with the world is enmity with God? Whoever therefore wants to be a friend of the world makes himself an enemy of God. or do you think that the Scripture says in vain, 'The Spirit who dwells in us yearns jealously'? But He gives more grace. Therefore He says: 'God resists the proud, but gives grace to the humble."* Although God resists the proud person, if he/she repents with a **sincere** spirit-heart, God will gladly receive his/her humble position and forgive him/her.

This means he/she would submit to God, not to the devil, **or** self-will. Always, always **and always** put God first in your life! Dare to be like Daniel, know your purpose, and then stand firm and true! Give **God** your time; see how much more you will accomplish in one day! Never, never and I say it again **never** forget the love God shows you each day. His mercy is new every day! Read Lamentations 3:22-23 and write it in this space so you'll remember it and rejoice in God!

The phrase "I'll look like a geek, be labeled as a Jesus freak or a weird-o" are in God's world a true compliment! As a teen or pre-teen or even a new babe in Christ, you may not like these titles, but God does! It proves we're doing what He tells us to do in Titus 2:14. Check it out, read then write it in this space.

Where it says "His own special people" in the old King James Version of the Bible it says "peculiar people." How wonderful to know God loves us when the world calls us weird—right? Will you dare to discipline yourself from this world and its attractions? If so, **when you can make a complete commitment to God**, write it here. His desire for you is to be honest with Him **and** yourself! If you can't do it now don't write anything—wait until you can.

Humility cures Worldliness

WOW! Now isn't that a headline that should appear in our daily newspapers? **Verses 7-10 "Therefore submit to God. Resist the devil and he will flee from you. Draw near to God and He will draw near to you. Cleanse your hands, you sinners and purify your hearts, you double-*

minded". [Undecided, can't make up ones mind on one thing.] "Lament and mourn and weep! Let your laughter be turned to mourning and your joy to gloom. 10 humble yourselves in the sight of the Lord, and He will ***lift*** *you* ***up****.*" Resist, what is it? If you are thinking on the lines of opposition, refusing to accept, or go along with the crowd, defy and to stand firm; you are thinking exactly what God's man, James, is saying here. Therefore **first** on the agenda is to **stand firmly** against anything that the devil or self-pride wants to do, say, or go! Ah! Does that mean you are submitted to God? Yes it does! And the second is so close behind, that it looks or appears to be the "how to do" in the resisting process… **draw near to God and** He will -----do what?

Did you say **He will draw near to you?** Now that's a WOW line! Are you feeling that joyful jubilant emotion we started this journey with? Me too! To <u>know</u> **Almighty God** in **all His splendor** loves us so much that He draws near, closer than close! Near enough to smell His sweet aroma! Why do you think it says to "**draw near to God",** and not **"God will draw near to you**" first? Could it be He wants it to be **our** choice? He did give us a free will, which means choice. He tells us what else is needed to show humbleness, which gets rid of pride. It was the custom of this era to show outer expressions of humility by weeping and washing of the hands. By doing so it showed true remorse. Sometimes I feel we need this more in our day and time. It is so easy to say, "Yeah, I'm sorry," without any emotions whatsoever. If we are sincere we need to show it in our conduct! Remember, pride produces strife humility produces peace and meekness of character. Dwell on that last phrase <u>"And He will lift you up".</u> Isn't that just like God to do something so wonderful! God's word warns us that <u>exalting ourselves</u> results in a fall, but <u>when we humble ourselves before God</u>, **He will do** the exalting and lifting up both in this world and in the next world. Always be swift to confess your sin! Nothing is more effective and humbling than admitting you have been wrong or sinned. This doesn't mean you announce to the world "I have sinned" but that you go to God and the other person you have sinned against and make it right. If it is in thought then it is to God alone that you confess to. Sometimes when we tell someone we are thinking bad of him or her it will not help, but hinder his or her growth in God. I thank God so much that He is the only one who reads my thoughts, that is why I begin my day with Ps. 19:14. I would encourage you to look it up and adopt it as your prayer too. I have given you space to write it here.

Do Not Judge a Brother/Sister:

Verse 11 "Do not speak evil of one another, brethren He who speaks evil of a brother and judges his brother, speaks evil of the law and judges the law. But if you judge the law, you are not a doer of the law but a judge. 12 There is one Lawgiver, who is able to save and to destroy. Who are you to judge another?" Does this mean we can't tell when a Christian person is a true Christian? No! We discovered in chapter 2 how we can know if someone is a true believer or bondservant of the Lord. These verses are telling us not to speak evil of that person or persons, judging in a manner such as God. God alone has the right to do judging. In this verse it is condemning other persons to hell for the way they walk in Christ. This is not our position as fellow Believers in Christ. Look up Matthew 7:1-5 read it out loud so you can hear yourself. What is Matthew referring to?

Jesus does not forbid opinions or the condemnation of wrongdoing, **but** He forbids us in condemning others. Which is a **spirit of faultfinding** that overlooks one's own shortcomings while assuming the role of supreme judge in regard to the sins of others. Yet, be aware of recognizing their "fruits" according to God's word. It is not our job to pass judgment by what we say about other Christians, but to leave it to God! We just discovered about the tongue; watch your words and attitude concerning other believers' walk. Knowing God needs to be our highest priority, then our relationships with one another. If we contain a good interaction or oneness with God it will produce within us the qualities of character that will build and sustain all our relationships. Does that mean we will agree one hundred percent with all believers? No! However, it also does not give us the permission to speak badly of them. James ends this chapter **not to boast about tomorrow's plans**. Verses 13-17

Verse 13 "Come now, you who say, 'Today or tomorrow we will go to such and such a city, spend a year there, buy and sell, and make a profit' 14 whereas you do not know what will happen tomorrow. For what is your life? It is even a vapor that appears for a little time and then vanishes away. 15 Instead you ought to say, 'If the Lord wills, we shall live and do this or that.' 16 But now you boast in your arrogance. All such boasting is evil. 17 Therefore, to him who knows to do good and does not do it, to him it is sin.".* Do these verses tell us we shouldn't plan our future, or set goals? No way! What God is telling us is that God knows our future and we need to consult Him. He knows the length of our life! Otherwise it is asserting authority above God and that is **boasting! Verses.17- We need to choose to do what is good and right, and not sin by not recognizing God holds our future. When we assert the complete authority of our life **without** consulting God it is as having an affair of worldliness --- for whom of the world consults God first? Did not Jesus consult His Father before he did or went any place? Read it for yourself in John 7:16-18, 12:49-50. In Luke 22:42 even at the time of his near death, he says, "Not **my will** but yours be done."

In a nutshell:

1. Don't forget the "I"-z and the "u"-z that cause warring within you.
2. If you are a friend of the world you are an enemy of God.
3. God resists the proud and gives grace to the humble.
4. In our humbleness before God He will lift us up. Bragging is not a part of the Christian walk. Arrogance is like a slap in God's face!
5. Do not speak evil of other Christians as in passing judgment.

6. Consult God before making an outline of your future, or goals.
7. Check your Spirit walk first! "*to him who knows to do good and does not do it, to him it is sin.*"

How to grow from this chapter study:

Pray, pray and pray! Make sure it's with a sincere heart clean and washed by the blood of the Lamb.

1. Check the motives, just as you check the oil in a lawnmower before using it. 2. Look up the word **humble, pride**, and **sin** in your concordance and write out the references on another sheet of paper then attach it to the end of this chapter. This is a self in depth study and a great place to go when you need a "spiritual" check-up.

Cross-references for chapter Fourteen:

Verse one *Rom 7:23,* ***Verse three-*** *Job 27:8,9 Ps 66:18* ***Verse four*** *1st John 2:15, Gal 1:4* ***Verse five-*** *Gen 6:5* ***Verse six*** *Prov. 3:34* ***Verse seven*** *Eph 4:27, 6:11* ***Verse eight*** *2nd Chron 15:2, Isa 1:16, 1st Peter 1:22* ***Verse nine*** *Matt 5:4* ***Verse ten*** *Job 22:29* ***Verse eleven*** *1st Peter 2:1-3 Matt 7:1-5* ***Verse twelve*** *Matt 10:28, Rom 14:4* ***Verse fourteen*** *Job 7:7,* ***Verse fifteen*** *Acts 18:21,* ***Verse sixteen*** *1st Cor 5:6* ***Verse seventeen*** *Luke 12:47*

Chapter Five

We have arrived at the milestone in our journey of James! Go ahead, give a Whoop EEE!!! You have been very good and faithful traveler sticking with this journey; you merit a pat on the back! [Give yourself one, or the person on your right if this has been a group study and your guide is okay with it.] This stage of our journey we'll be discovering how **not** to seek or accumulate riches, a **true** Christians' behavior, and giving of ourselves to others in need. At one point the rich were getting richer by oppressing the Christian Jews by withholding their pay. They were hoarding money, now that sounds familiar doesn't it? Practical James, he is so likable in how he presents these issues of his time as well as for our modern day world! My fervent prayer throughout this designated time will be that you will continue *praying* passionately, **extend** your *faith* in all circumstances in your life and **commit** to being a *bondservant* to Jesus Christ! James has given us great instructions on these things through the Holy Spirit.

Are you ready to get digging for new discoveries? Okay!

Lets get digging!

Rich Oppressors Will Be Judged

*Verse 1-6 *"Come now, **you rich**, weep and howl for your miseries that are coming upon you! 2 Your riches are corrupted, and your garments are moth-eaten. 3 Your gold and silver are corroded and their corrosion will be a witness against you and will eat your flesh like fire. You have heaped up treasure in the last days. 4 Indeed the wages of the laborers who mowed your fields, which you kept back by fraud, cry out; and the cries of the* *reapers have reached the ears of the Lord of Sabaoth. [Hebrew for Host] 5 You have lived on the earth in pleasure and luxury; you have fattened your hearts as in a day of slaughter. 6 You have condemned, you have murdered the just; he does not resist you."* What do you feel James is expressing in the passage above?

If you feel money is completely out of the picture for a **bondservant of Jesus Christ**, you need to check out what is really being said. However if you say that the servant of Jesus Christ needs to be careful how **they acquire** money you are correct. Always be objective how you **receive** payment for what you do, as well as **if you owe,** be sure to **pay justly** what is owed! Make sure money doesn't **control you** but **you control it**. Sometimes the things God gives us will begin to rule our life. That is when we go Ker-plop! Stumble and fall spiritually into the same place these people did. [Remember check your motive gauge.] James is talking about fraud, and with fraud judgment is sure to come! It may not be through the court system, but God who sees all will be the just and perfect Judge and render what is due to those who oppress or cheat others. That is why these rich were warned to weep and howl because they would without doubt face God's just judgment! They had cheated for self gain! What happens when we cheat? Yes indeed, in the long run of life we are cheating ourselves! We don't have peace, joy or any of the rest of the Fruits of the Spirit! It's comforting to know that God sees and hears those who have been cheated --- re-read verse four. What is it saying to **you?** James is encouraging all Christians to embrace the **simple** life in Christ. He is not saying you need to be in **poverty**! There is a huge difference in a life of simplicity and one of poverty. It's like a big cavern between the two life styles! Do you know the difference? Write it here:

Simplicity is:

____

Poverty is:

____

If you said simplicity is acting responsible with what God has given you, then you are correct. And if you said Poverty is needy or living in hardship, you are correct again! God never asked for His people to be in want, or David would never have said of God in Psalm 37:25 "I have been young, and now am old; yet I have not seen the **righteous forsaken**, nor his descendants **begging for bread**." [In need] Jesus in the sample prayer given to His disciples says in Matt. 6:11 *"Give us this **day** our **daily bread."*** Look up Philippians 4:19 read and then write it here:

____

____

Does that sound like God wants us to live in poverty? No-way! Be blessed and use what God has given you to bless not only yourself but also those He puts in your life! Keep in mind, it may not always be money, it may be talents or time, whatever it is, be sure to give it **all** to Jesus and He will bless you! Looking forward to the next six verses will give us hope. We are encouraged to **be Patient and Persevering.**

Verse 7-12 "Therefore be patient, brethren, until the coming of the Lord. See how the farmer waits for the precious fruit of the earth, waiting patiently for it until it receives the early and latter rain. 8 You also be patient. Establish your hearts, for the coming of the Lord is at hand. 9 <u>Do not grumble against one another, brethren, lest you be condemned. Behold, the Judge is standing at the door.</u> 10 My brethren, take the prophets, who spoke in the name of the Lord as an example of suffering and patience. 11 Indeed we count them blessed who endure. You have heard of the perseverance of Job and seen the end intended by the Lord—that the Lord is very compassionate and merciful. 12 But above all, my brethren<u>, do not swear</u>, either by heaven or by earth or with any other oath. But let your "Yes" be "Yes" and your "No" be "No", lest you fall into judgment."* In verse seven James is encouraging believers, not to give up hope. Patience is what is needed just as a farmer has to wait for his crop to produce, so it is with the coming of Jesus the righteous Judge! When He does come God will fulfill or execute justice to all. Faithful to His word, He will reward the just, and execute judgment or punishment to the wicked. It makes my heart sing with joy knowing God sees all hearts! No pretenders, no hypocrites, and no deceivers, will ever fool God! They may fool us, with good works, big smiles, and a bubbly disposition, but they will not fool God! In verse nine I underlined it to call your full attention to it. Does it not say we are **not to grumble about our Brethren? In the literal meaning it says *not to groan*, and in the Paraphrased Living Bible it says, "*Don't grumble about each other, brothers. Are you yourselves above* ***criticism?***" Haven't we heard that in this journey before? It is so easy to pass judgment or criticize others, but God wants for us to refrain from such actions. It is for Him and Him only to judge or criticize. The following statement James continues, "*see or behold, the Judge is standing at the door.*" In this statement we must remember what **Peter** has to say about the coming of Jesus in **2nd Peter 3:8-10**. Also in this passage Peter tells you how to determine what a day or year is like to God. Lets look it up, and then write it here so you will never forget that God is not slack, or slow, in His coming and Judgment.

____

____

Now to make verses ten and eleven come alive to you turn to **Hebrews 11** in your Bible. It will paint a picture for you how a true believer walks out their faith and the reward that follows! Like-wise if we persevere [never give up] through our sufferings we too will receive

God's justice and rewards. Morals in this era have deteriorated where a few dedicated believers, or followers of God, take His word serious. It is a must in order to be called a **true** Bondservant of Christ Jesus. Therefore if you hold morals and honesty a priority and holiness in high regards be prepared to be ridiculed! Suffering today for Christ's sake will vary from being snubbed, unpopular, and in a few cases disowned.

However, remember that Jesus is worth it all. He gave His all-why can't we give ours to Him?

I see a great "side path, lets take it and discover something about the people in Hebrews chapter 11, and what their life was like. Following are the names of these prophets/special people, put next to it what they were known for and how we need to be like them. Hebrews 11

Person of Faith, what did he/she **believe for**?	What was this person **known for?**	**What I can learn from this person's faith.**
Abel: Vs.4		
Enoch: Vs.5		
Noah: Vs.7		
Abraham: Vs.8		
Sarah: Vs. 11		
Isaac: Vs.20		
Jacob: Vs.21		
Joseph: Vs.22		
Moses' parents: Vs.23		
Moses: Vs.24		
The people of Israel Vs.27-30		
Rahab: Vs. 31		

Fill in the blanks.

****Verse 32 –Living Bible "Well, how much more do I need to say? It would take too long to recount the stories of the faith of: 1+____________________ and ____________________ and ____________________ and ____________________ and ____________________ and ____________________ the other ____________________." Did you like discovering these people on this side trip? How would you have felt if God had asked you to do some of these things? Write your comments in this space.

____

In my opinion here, God wants us to know without a doubt, it's **doing** the His will as well as **knowing** or merely **believing** that He **<u>is!</u>** **Facts** are **facts,** it **is our choice** to <u>know,</u> <u>believe and **do**</u> what we have discovered on being a true Christian. Think about it seriously, we call our self a Christian; do you see the first part of that word? **Christ**'? Why then would we deliberately smear His name by our language, and behavior? We can learn volumes of truth and be encouraged if we will learn from these faithful few listed above.

Then just like these prophets of old, we too will see and say, "The Lord is very compassionate and merciful." Doesn't that make the jubilant juices within you want to shout ---- YEAH-HOOOO? Then lets do it! YEAH-HOOOOOOO!

Perhaps that is difficult for you to identify with a God who loves so deeply and completely, that it is confusing to you. If you don't have or haven't experienced a family history that goes back to the faithful, submitted, and persevering family ties, God wants to heal all those hurts. Know first of all that there are many others that have walked that path before you. Take Rahab, it doesn't look like there were a lot of family that pursued a faithful walk with God, yet look how God used her not only to deliver herself from death, but her entire family. Why? Simply because she **believed** and **<u>acted</u>** upon that faith in the Israelites' God! God will do the same for you, my dear traveling partner of God's word! He has no favorites! Acts 10:34 & 35 read and write in your own words what it tells you here.

____

____

Now back on the trail with James we will consider in depth what **patience** and **perseverance** is. It wasn't only James that spoke on this subject Paul in his letter to Timothy in 1st Timothy 6:11says; *"But you, O man of God, flee these things and pursue righteousness, godliness, faith, love,* ***patience****, gentleness."* What was Timothy to pursue? The fifth attribute is what? ____________________. Why do you think it fell in the fifth position? Could it be when righteousness, godliness, faith and love are in control that it would be much more likely that patience and gentleness would be close behind? Can you think of a moment when God has shown you His patience? I'll leave some space so you can write it and recall it often.

____

When you hear the word patience, what do you think of? Perhaps someone that has shown you gentle guidance, or continued forgiveness, or staying power. When was the last time you showed patience with someone? Lets take a moment now to talk about **persevere**. First how would you define it?

____

If you said to be persistent, keep trying, not to give up easily or continue, you have said correctly. My father told me that as a small kid I was stubborn. When I was going through some very hard life trials I was chatting with my father and asked him if he thought I was being stubborn, or perseverant concerning a certain situation? He replied, "perseverant, I reckon I need to reconsider that was what you were as a kid too, now that I take a good look at the two words" How my heart leaped for joy and gladness in his answer! After making a full study of the two words, I realized why I didn't like the word stubborn. Stubborn in my opinion gives a negative selfish immoveable attitude where to be persistent is holding true to ones convictions. When were the last time you had to be perseverant, or holding fast to that what you knew was the right thing to do?

Good for you for holding true to your convictions! Traveling on now to the next issue James is talking about: **Meeting Specific Needs:** *Verses 13-18 "*Is anyone among you suffering? Let him pray. Is anyone cheerful? Let him sing psalms. 14 Is anyone among you sick? Let him call for the elders* [officers] *of the church, and let them pray over him, anointing him with oil* [symbolic of the Holy Spirit not literally medicinal oil Mark 6:13] *in the name of the Lord. 15 and the prayer of the faith* [referring to the faith the Holy Spirit gives in connection with God almighty 1st Corinthians 12:9] *will save the sick, and the Lord will raise him up. And if he has committed sins, he will be forgiven. 16 Confess your trespasses to one another, and pray for one another, that you may be healed. The effective, fervent prayer of the righteous man avails much. 17 Elijah was a man with a nature like ours, and he prayed earnestly that it would not rain; and it did not rain on the land for three years and six months.*

18 And he prayed again, and the heaven gave rain, and the earth produced its fruit." Why is it so seldom we hear the truth behind this collection of truths? Doctor Jesus has given us a "prescription" for every situation we face yet the majority of His bondservants neglect in following or filling that prescription! [yes, me included]! Are you suffering right now? Here's your chance to **do** God's Word – look at it again. "*Let **him** pray.*" What is that prayer to be like? Check out Philippians 4:6 that prayer is to be **with** a thankful heart, or an attitude of gratitude. Psalm 50:14, 15 explains it like this "Offer to God, **thanksgiving**, ***Word Wealth** : explains **thanksgiving** in this verse as: adoration, praise. The word is derived or developed from the verb *yadah*, meaning "to give thanks", "to praise". And the root of *yadah* is *yad*, "hand." To thank or praise God by lifting or extend one's hands in thanks to Him. Take time; if you are suffering to do this **now!** Allow it to be a WOW time in this study-time. I've been suffering with a sore/ stiff neck for almost a week and a half. I took time to offer God thanks during this writing and worshiped and praised Him and yes! True to His Word, my neck is no longer sore or stiff! WOW! It's difficult to type when my brain keeps praising God, I want to repeat the praises here… like glory! Awesome God! Almighty! Most high God! I love you Lord! Praise your Holy name, Jesus! The LORD IS an awesome God, and king above all kings!

I wish to tell you about one young traveler during our class time. Her back had been hurting her severely. So as her troop leader we stopped our study right here and reread the scripture. I said "the **Word** says if **any one is suffering let him/her pray**, then I asked if she would put her hands on the area that hurt, and we'd be praising God (quietly) while she prayed for herself. With her eyes closed and a sincere look upon her face she placed her hands on her low back and in a quiet voice made her request for God to take the pain from her back so she could do the things she needed to. As I observed her face it was like a small flicker of a smile and then her eyes popped open and a huge grin and a laugh that was so joyful the rest of us in the room began laughing and praising God for her healing! It was a **wow** moment, that's why I encourage you not to rush through this part of your trip, don't miss a blessed treasure! Plus Kendra at eleven years old will forever remember this moment and God's hands upon her. It would be a good time now or later to read Psalm 95 known as Call to Worship and Obedience Psalm. Wait before the almighty and rejoice with a great shout of joy! Now write it here what God almighty has done for you.

You may already know that in Hebrew "Jehovah" is God almighty" and Jehovah-Rapha is God my healer. He is the physical and emotional doctor desiring to meet all the needs of <u>His people</u>! Use it my friend, He desires for you to walk in His Word, not just read it and say, "isn't that nice" or "that makes me feel **so** good!" **No**! That **will not** produce the bondservant He desires! He **longs** to make you complete! *Jesus was Jehovah –Rapha, in healing the sick, blind, lame, and even casting out demons. And Jesus also heals His people from sin and all unrighteousness. Read these following scriptures and make a short to the point note of what it says.

Luke 5:31,32
1st John 1:9
Psalm 103:3 -5
Psalm 147:3-6
1st Peter 2:24

After all that wonderful excitement of walking in the Word, are you ready to tackle the next few prescriptions [instructions] God has given us to fill? Good! *Are you cheerful? <u>Let</u> him sing.* Are you cheerful today? Then take time to sing praises to God! Doesn't it say to **<u>let</u>** <u>him sing</u>? Let means to allow, give right of way, so sing! It doesn't matter if you carry a tune or not, make a joyful noise unto him, worship and adore Him with all your might, soul and strength! Ephesians 5:19 says: *"speaking to one another in psalms and hymns and spiritual songs, <u>singing and making melody</u> in* ***your*** *<u>heart to the Lord".</u>* To whom? Yes, the Lord! So it doesn't matter if you have a gorgeous voice! Ps.100:1 and Ps.95:1-3 calls it a joyful shout! What song of praise or joyful shout comes to your mind at this particular time? My heart began singing my favorite *"Great is the Lord, and greatly to be praised, in the city of my God in the mountain of His holiness*" Psalm 48:1. And "*What an Awesome God I serve"* Ps. 47:1 and 2. Next question, *"is anyone sick"*? What is the prescription? Write it here ____________________ Verse 15: What is the result when the sick fill the Great Physician's prescription? Write it here.

____

*Verse 16 It sounds like another Prescription to me, read it and see what you think. *"Therefore, confess your sins, or trespasses to one another and pray for one another, that you may be healed. The effective, fervent prayer of a righteous man* [person] *avails much."* This is not a confession before the church of what sin that was committed, but to the one to whom it was committed against. Be it slander, or gossip or perhaps you took something from someone, what is that called? OH, yes, that is stealing! And notice too, back in verse 15, which is tied into this that **if** he has committed sins--- he will be healed and verse 16 is likewise, to **pray** as well as **confess** one to another, which in turn produces a great environment for God to work His prescription or instructions to us, and *you will be healed.* Why? Could it be because God is faithful? God, through his bondservant, James, finished off that thought with these words, *"the effective, fervent prayer of a righteous man avails much."* Explain the words +1 Effective ____________________ and +2 fervent ____________________. In some translations of the Bible the word fervent is also translated supplication. What does that word mean? +3 ____________________. James gave us a good example of a righteous man in the last verse in this section. Elijah was well known in his day. What does verses seventeen and eighteen have to say of him? Indeed, he was just like we are, he had his weaknesses, and his strengths like all humans. Yet when he prayed earnestly, or fervently, what happened? 1+ ____________________ 2+ ____________________ Let's take a side path and discover what this trail marked 1st Kings 17:1 is all about. Here's another trail, 1st Kings 18:1 what are the results here? 3+ ____________________ God answered Elijah to show the wayward Israelites and Ahab that God is alive and well in His kingdom! Sometimes I'm totally amazed at God's patience with humans! He's God, yet he proves it many times that humans will know that He is whom He says! Sometime you may want to come back to this trail and discover all kinds of wonders, remember it's called 1st Kings 18:20-40. What a wonderful work of faith and victory! My map, or Bible, on our last and final trail on this journey is how to bring back the erring or one who has strayed **Bringing Back the Erring One. Ready to discover how? Lets get digging.** **Verse 19-20 "brethren, if anyone among you wanders from the truth, and someone turns him back, 20 let him know that he who turns a* ***sinner*** *from the error of his way will save a soul from death and cover a multitude of sins."* Did you notice I underlined "brethren if anyone among you" and "turns him back"? Good, the purpose for doing that was to cause you to think about it. What do you think it is expressing (1+) ____? How can you turn someone back to Jesus if they haven't wander away from their faith in Jesus? You can't! Therefore, it means a church member, or follower of Jesus Christ. This doesn't mean you watch for believers to stumble or pick on someone that has different convictions from yours, but when and if that person takes on a behavior or characteristic of sin. What is sin? Remember, we discussed that before. It is **willfully going against** what God has told us to do in His Word, the Bible, or our map for Christian living. Let's think of someone you may know that has done this. Have you confronted that person(s)? If the answer is yes, then you must allow the **Holy Spirit** to do **His** work. Remember, not one of us **is** the Holy Spirit, although we have him in our life! We are to be the channel in which God flows to aid that one who is slipping away from godly principles and behavior. Hopefully Love is the motivation in addressing the issue(s) showing God's love, not being condemning or better than them. I would say if you were following the Holy Spirit in what you say or do it would come out in a godly way. Keep in mind that person(s) has to make the decision to change, **not** you! You are **not** their conscience, **not** their free will, nor their **judge**; you may **not** even be a friend to chum with. You may be related, you may have known them for a very long time, but if that person(s) passion is to do what **they** want, there is nothing more you can do, outside of forgiving and praying for them. The reason I put forgiving them first is because I felt the Holy Spirit telling me how can one pray earnestly or fervently for someone's sick spirit if you haven't forgiven them? Yes, indeed they posses a sick spirit to decide to go back into sin once they have known the Word of God! This so often brings separation of friendships and sometimes family. Why? Because what does light have to do with darkness? Read Jn 3:19-21, 1st Jn 1:7, and Eph 5:8. Then finish it with Eph 5:7. What do these scriptures tell you? Write it in your own paraphrase and remember to do it!

1. Jn. 3:19-21-
2. 1st Jn. 1:7-
3. Eph. 5:8-
4. Eph. 5:7-

It takes the Holy Spirit to help you confront such a one, please save yourself a ton of anguish and talk to that person when **you know** it is **God's Spirit** that is leading and not you spouting your feelings. Take it from me, it doesn't work! Regretfully, I found out the hard way. Nobody took time to mentor me when I first became a Christian so I went through spiritual training via the school of "hard knocks" for my Christian growth. I still pray God will help those I tried to in my way, not His way. Let's stray again, these side paths are quit interesting don't you think? Check your map on trail 2nd Timothy 2:15. What does it say we're to do? Some translations will say to study, others say be diligent and still others say work hard, yet they basically say the same thing, know the Word of God! God calls us in this passage a "worker." I'm sure you have at some time watched ants. That is how we are to be with our Lord and Savior Jesus Christ. Always striving to please him! Read it again and notice that a worker who does not need to be ashamed, rightly dividing the word of truth. In order to rightly divide the word we first must know it! * 'Paul uses the metaphors of an unashamed workman, a clean vessel, and a gentle servant to illustrate the Christian minister.

Christian minister is one that mentors, or is walking in Christ! Standing firm upon what God is saying, not doing what others want or think you should do, where you should go, or the language you use, how you dress your body the temple of the Holy Spirit. All this side tracking to express how important it is to **know** God's word and Him personally, how else can we help those we see giving up on walking the trail with Jesus? Dear fellow trekker some day when our days are gone here on earth we shall hear God saying to us, "well done my faithful hiker, come home to Me"! Ahhh, the older I get the sweeter those words are becoming. Yet it is so exciting to feel His spirit moving and leading me here too… I guess I am like Paul the apostle when he says "For me to live is Christ, and to die is gain" Philippians 1:21. Back on the main trail with James once again, we'll discover what **sinners** in verse twenty is talking about. In the Spirit Filled Life Bible, sinners is in bold type and explained as follows: "One that misses the mark, a traveler leaving the familiar road and taking a twisted path that **causes him** to **lose his way**. The word denotes one devoted to sin **by choice**, a transgressor whose **thoughts, words, and deeds** are **contrary** to the eternal laws of God." A person makes **a choice** to either walk in God's Word, live by faith and in God's grace or to walk in ones **own choices** in life, creating for ones self a selfish and prideful path. In conclusion, *'the **soul** and the **sins** covered are those of the one restored. By bringing the erring one to repentance and confession, forgiveness is obtained! What a wonderful thought to close this journey, wouldn't you say? I pray you are overjoyed for the great choice you made in taking this journey. I also pray you will take many more and dwell in the presence of the glorious Father above.

In a Nutshell:

1. Be sure not to be deceitfulness to anyone lest you reap judgment.
2. Be patient just like a farmer is when you plant seeds for God. The word needs to be watered and tended to just as any food crop.

3. **<u>Do not fear suffering for Christ</u>**! He gave his all; I need to also give to Him my all.
4. Above all <u>watch your language</u>, do not swear.
5. <u>Jesus prescriptions</u>/instructions when you suffer- are joyful- sick- all in verses 13-15.
6. How <u>to pray and get results</u> from praying verse 16.
7. Allow the <u>Holy Spirit to flow through you</u> to help one that has fallen or chosen to sin.
8. <u>Relax in Christ</u>; it is He in us that will do the working of the Word!

How to grow from this chapter study:

1. Take each one of the old testament characters listed in this chapter starting on Page 45 and study what their life was about, not just one or two verses but their entire life. Then set your goal to do likewise.
2. Just because it's the end of the journey, don't walk away and forget what ground you have traveled, but claim each step in a forever new, walk with your Savior, and Lord.
3. Now pass on, or share, through the Holy Spirit's leading, your knowledge of what a true Christian **is** and how they **live** each beautiful day.
4. The awesome power, authority, we have as the **"church"** standing <u>together</u> to help one another.
5. Never, and I repeat that **never** think you have learned it all, keep discovering /studying to be an approved workman, or bondservant to Jesus!

Cross-references for this chapter:

Verse one Luke 6:24 **Verse two** Matt. 6:19, Job 13:28 **Verse three** Rom 2:5 **Verse four** Lev.19: 13, Deut. 24:15 **Verse ten** Matt. 5:12, Heb. 10:36 **Verse eleven** Ps. 94:12, Matt. 5:10, James 1:2, Job 1:21-22, 2:10, 42:10, Numbers 14:18 **Verse twelve** Matt. 5:34-37 **Verse thirteen**.

Ps.50: 14-15, Eph. 5:19 **Verse fourteen** Mark 6:13, 16:18 **Verse fifteen** Isa. 33:24 **Verse sixteen**. Num 11:2 **Verse seventeen.** Acts 14:15, 1st Kings 17:1, 18:1 **Verse eighteen** 1st Kings 18:1, 42 **Verse nineteen**. Matt. 18:15, Gal. 6:1, and **Verse twenty**. Rom. 11:14, 1st Cor. 1:21 Jam.1: 21 Pro. 10:12

My evaluation of this journey for my life is:

What have I learned?

What I need to change:

My prayer of commitment:

I reviewed this study on these dates; noting briefly my changes each time:

Thesauruses definitions

for specific words in chapter five

Chapter five

+1 Pg.51 **Effective**: Operative, active, working, and functioning

+2 Pg.51 **Fervent:** Eager, intense, wholehearted, dedicated.

+3 Pg.51 **Supplication:** plea, petition, request, appeal, and demand- as using Scripture to back up the demand, "it is written" such as Jesus used when tempted of Satan. The Greek meaning is "Having energy"

Answer to blanks sheet for:

Chapter five

Pg 46 1+ **blank answers**: Gideon, Barak, Samson, Jephthah, David, Samuel, all Prophets.

Pg 51 1+ **blank answers:** God answered him, +2 No rain, +3 it rained.

Pg 52 1+ **blank answers:** A member of the Church.

Pg 58 1+ **blank answers** present oneself approved

A Word From The Transcriber:

I WANT YOU TO know we all fall down, make mistakes, and we will as long as we are on planet earth. However, God is in the business of forgiveness, so as soon as you hear the Holy Spirit speaking to you concerning your mistake, or sin, confess it and get back on track. Be blessed for I truly have been blessed in being submissive to the Holy Spirit's leading in preparing this study manual. Never can I understand nor want to under estimate how God's Spirit uses a Bondservant of His. He is truly awesome! That is why when I have things like this published I use a "writer's name" because I do not want to give the devil or pride in me to say, "look at my accomplishment." Only a few that knew how God called me to do this will know---and I leave it at that!

One thing I wish to pass along to you dear dedicated learners is this:

if you feel at a loss and don't know how to do something, whatever it may be, the Holy Spirit knows exactly how to accomplish that particular task. He was sent to the world to "Teach, Guide, and Comfort" each one of us, so don't hesitate in asking Him how to do whatever it is you need! My favorite phrase is "Help me **today Lord** to do and say what **you** want done or said. Plan my day, thank you Father!" There will be adult bondservants in a local church that would be delighted to help you too, so open up and grow in your Spirit-life. Ignorance is not bliss!

Perhaps you don't have a Church family. Who gave you this manual, or invited you to attend a Bible study? I'm sure they would be very pleased to have you join them in their fellowship of believers.

Praise Him All the Time and you will be victorious!

Autobiography

For Abigail J. EnWhite

ONE DAY WHEN I was five and in the "punishing closet" l encountered Jesus in a dream. However, I kept it a secret because I had a stuttering defect and I had learned in Sunday school from the stories of Joseph that it doesn't pay to tell your secrets to family members. I was twelve when I made it known during a revival service at my church that I wanted Jesus as my Savior. In my journey I have encountered desert-dry situations, as well as some fun and lighthearted situations. Believe me, it was the desert places that taught me lessons I would never forget! I had no place to turn apart from Jesus for help, comfort or wisdom. For this I am forever grateful because Jesus is the only one that cares 100% of the time. Sixty-four years ago my commitment to Jesus has grown to the point where I do nothing without His okay and peace upon the situation. My story telling years began early in life to my two sisters I shared my sleeping area with. In high school I would write other students essays. I'm sure they needed a lot of correction but the one requesting and receiving the work done were quite happy! In 1980 I received a diploma for writing for children, teens and adults. This was a huge encouragement because two years before the diploma arrived I lost my husband and learned what trusting God was all about. The details of that loss don't matter, all that matters is I passionately desired to become b**e**tter not b**i**tter; —one small letter that makes a world of difference in not only **my** journey but also those God so graciously has had me travel with. In 2008 I joined christianwriters.com for a short season and received valuable support. However the greatest experience of all is listening and waiting for God's Holy Spirit then allowing Him to guide me as I write! As of this writing I have seven grandchildren each so much a blessing. I treasure their lives and pray they too will long for and gain knowledge and wisdom for their Spirit-life.

Enjoying my journey and reaching out to the lost or the new traveler in Christ.